How to Increase Business Profits

A Step By Step Plan to Increase
the Profitability of Your Company

By Meir Liraz

Published by BizMove
www.bizmove.com

ISBN: 9781090319531

Table of Contents

MEIR LIRAZ

1. Basics of Profit Planning

Profit planning, increasing your business profit, is simply the development of your operating plan for the coming period. Your plan is summarized in the form of an income statement that serves as your sales and profit objective and your budget for cost.

How Is It Used?

Profit planning is used in the following ways:

Evaluating operations. Each time you prepare an income statement, actual sales and costs are compared with those you projected in your original profit plan. This permits detection of areas of unsatisfactory performance so that corrective action can be taken.

Determining the need for additional resources such as facilities or personnel. For example, the profit plan may show that a sharp increase in expected sales will overload the company's billing personnel. A decision can then be made to add additional invoicing personnel, to retain an EDP service, or to pursue some other alternative.

Planning purchasing requirements. The volume of expected sales may be more than the business' usual suppliers can handle or expected sales may be sufficient to permit taking advantage of quantity discounts. In either case, advance knowledge of purchasing requirements will permit taking advantage of cost savings and ensure that purchased goods are readily available when needed.

Anticipating any additional financing needs. With planning, the search for needed funds can begin as early as possible. In this way, financial crises are avoided and financing can be arranged on more favorable terms.

Advantages of Profit Planning

Profit planning offers many advantages to your business. The modest investment in time required to develop and implement the plan will pay liberal dividends later. Among the benefits that your business can enjoy from profit planning are the following:

Performance evaluation. The profit plan provides a continuing standard against which sales performance and cost control can quickly be evaluated.

Awareness of responsibilities. With the profit plan, personnel are readily aware of their responsibilities for meeting sales objectives, controlling costs, and the like.

Cost consciousness. Since cost excesses can quickly be identified and planned, expenditures can be compared with budgets even before they are incurred, cost consciousness is increased, reducing unnecessary costs and overspending.

Disciplined approach to problem-solving. The profit plan permits early detection of potential problems so that their nature and extent are known. With this information, alternate corrective actions can be more easily and accurately evaluated.

Thinking about the future. Too often, small businesses neglect to plan ahead: thinking about where they are today, where they will be next year, or the year after. As a result, opportunities are overlooked and crises occur that could have been avoided. Development of the profit plan requires thinking about the future so that many problems can be avoided before they arise.

Financial planning. The profit plan serves as a basis for financial planning. With the information developed from the profit plan, you can anticipate the need for increased investment in receivables, inventory, or facilities as well as any need for additional capital.

Confidence of lenders and investors. A realistic profit plan, supported by a description of specific steps proposed to achieve sales and profit objectives, will inspire the confidence of potential lenders and investors. This confidence will not only influence their judgment of you as a business manager, but also the prospects of your business' success and its worthiness for a loan or an investment.

Limitations of Profit Planning

Profit plans are based upon estimates. Inevitably, many conditions you expected when the plan was prepared will change. Crystal balls are often cloudy. The further down the road one attempts to forecast, the cloudier they become. In a year, any number of factors can change, many of them beyond the control of the company. Customers' economic fortunes may decline, suppliers' prices may increase, or suppliers' inability to deliver may disrupt your plan.

The profit plan requires the support of all responsible par?ties. Sales quotas must be agreed upon with those responsible for meeting them. Expense budgets must be agreed upon with the people who must live with them. Without mutual agreement on objectives and budgets, they will quickly be ignored and serve no useful purpose.

Finally, profit plans must be changed from time to time to meet changing conditions. There is no point in trying to operate a business according to a plan that is no longer realistic because conditions have changed.

Advantages vs. Disadvantages

Despite the limitations of profit planning, the advantages far outweigh the disadvantages. A realistic plan, established yearly and reevaluated as changing conditions require will provide performance guidelines that will help you control every aspect of your business with a minimum of analysis and digging for financial facts.

Guide Objectives

In this guide, you will learn how to do the following:

Develop a forecast for sales and gross profit, considering all of the various internal and external factors that are relevant to the forecast.

Develop budgets for operating expenses to quickly detect excessive expenses so that corrective action can be taken and purchasing commitments held within budgetary limits.

Estimate net profit so that you can determine whether or not the projected return on your investment is satisfactory. You will also be able to determine how much cash will be generated from operations either for reinvestment in the business or to compensate owners for their investment.

2. How to Forecast your Sales And Gross Profit

Development of your profit plan should usually begin with a forecast of your expected sales and gross profit for the coming year. The sales and gross profit must be considered together since they are so closely interrelated. Gross profit percentages are determined by pricing policy, which also affects expected sales volume. A decision to increase the expected gross profit percentage will usually tend to decrease expected sales, while reducing the expected gross profit percentage should increase sales.

A second major reason for beginning the profit plan with a sales forecast is that the volume of expected sales often determines a number of other factors such as the following:

Expected changes in variable expenses, those expenses that tend to change in direct proportion to changes in sales. These could include expenses such as sales commissions or delivery costs.

The impact of the added sales volume on the various fixed costs of operating your business. These costs, by definition, do not tend to vary in direct proportion to changes in sales volume. However, substantial increases in sales over an extended period can force an increase in many fixed expenses. For example, a sales increase realized through the addition of many new accounts could affect bookkeeping and credit costs.

The ability of present resources such as storage space, display area, delivery capability, or supervisory personnel to accommodate the added volume.

The need for funds to invest in increased inventory or accounts receivable to accommodate sales increases.

Cash generated from operations to meet current operating needs as well as expansion requirements, debt repayments, and owners' compensation.

Realism

A realistic sales forecast must rely on careful analysis of market potential and the ability of your business to capture its share of this potential. The forecast should not be based upon "what you would like to do" or "what you hope to do." It must be "what you can do" and "what you will do."

Any forecast of a sales increase must be supported by realistic expectations for stronger market demand and specific marketing steps that will be taken to capture a share of this market.

The key to successful forecasting is realism. You only fool yourself if you reject reality in forecasting. Such fore?casts serve neither as a realistic planning basis nor as a reliable means of performance evaluation.

Your forecast can be the basis for important decisions such as decisions to add personnel, lease additional facilities, or increase promotional costs. If these decisions are based upon unrealistic sales expectations, any money expended on them will be wasted.
Forecasts are often presented to lenders or potential investors to guide them in their decisions. If they lack confidence in your forecast, they will certainly be reluctant to commit their funds to your business.

Every forecast should be supported by carefully considered, specific action plans. It is inadequate to forecast a sales increase of 20% or 30% without plans for specific actions to achieve the increase. These actions could include the introduction of new products, opening of new branches, market expansion, commitments from new customers, increased requirements from existing customers, additional salesmen, or an intensified promotional effort to attract new customers.

Analyzing Current Sales and Gross Profit

Your sales and gross profit forecast begins with analysis of current performance. Sales are usually divided into various categories. Each category is examined individually to determine expected sales for the coming year.

Selecting Sales Categories

The selection of categories will depend upon the nature of your business. For example, a food broker selling to a large number of relatively small accounts might be interested primarily in analyzing sales by product. The owner of a single retail store might choose to analyze sales by selling department, while the owner of a retail chain would probably be interested in analyzing sales by outlet. An insurance broker with several agents might categorize sales by agent. An individual wholesaler might consider sales by sales territory.

Factors Affecting Sales

After categories have been selected and current sales divided among them, the various factors which can affect sales in each category must be considered. These factors could be either internal or external. Internal factors are those that you can influence. External factors are those that affect the market served by your business, but are generally beyond your control.

Internal Factors

The following are typical internal factors that could influence your sales forecast:

Promotional plans

Expansion plans

Capacity restrictions

New product introductions

Product cancellations

Sales force changes

Pricing policy

Profit expectations

Market expansion to new customers or territories

External Factors

Among the external factors that must be considered are the following:

Business trends

Government policies

Inflation

Changes in population characteristics

Economic fortunes of customers

Changes in buying habits

Competitive pressures

Analyzing Gross Profit Percentages

It is often useful to begin a sales forecast with an examination of your current gross profit percentage (markup percentage or gross profit percentage). The gross profit percentage is usually the best indicator of pricing policy which can have significant impact on sales volume. To some extent, the gross profit percentage will also reflect the buying economies of your business. However, the range over which costs of purchased goods will vary is not ordinarily as wide as the possible range of prices you may seek for your products.

Three Bases of Comparison

Examination of current gross profit percentages can indicate the need for pricing policy revisions to meet competition or closer attention to purchasing costs in order to provide extra gross profit without increasing prices.

The evaluation of gross profit percentages requires comparison of current performance with three bases:

Objectives originally set for the current year, if available

Other businesses in the same industry

Results of prior years

Comparison with objectives permits you to determine how well you have done compared with your original expectations. Assuming that these objectives were realistic, this is often the best single performance indicator. Deviations from objectives can quickly be identified and explored in detail to determine the cause of the deviation.

Comparison with industry averages permits identification of areas where the experience of similar businesses indicates room for improvement in your own.

Unfortunately, businesses are often too quick to dismiss the applicability of industry averages to their own operation, claiming that "Our circumstances are different." Such an attitude is self-defeating. It prevents you from taking advantage of the experience of others to improve your own sales and profit. A far more productive attitude is to say, "If everybody else can realize a gross profit of x percent, then we should be able to." Until specific circumstances are identified that make it impossible for your business to be consistent with industry averages, every attempt should be made to bring performance in line with the experience of others.

Comparison of current operations with performance in prior periods permits detection of trends so that progress, or the lack of it, can be identified. It also permits evaluation in light of those specific considerations that may be unique to your business. For example, if your gross profit as a percentage of sales is low compared with the industry, analysis of your historic performance may reveal the cause of this apparent deficiency such as reliance upon a major customer where severe competition restricts the available gross profit percentage.

Evaluating Gross Profit Percentages

Refer to the table below, which is an analysis of gross profit percentages realized by Western Appliances in the year XXX2. Percentages are shown for cost of sales, gross profit, total expenses, and profit before taxes as follows:

XXX2 actual

XXX1 actual

Industry average

XXX2 objective

Each basis of comparison provides a different viewpoint of the company's operations.

WESTERN APPLIANCES, INC.
Profit Percentage Analysis

	XXX2 actual	XXX1 actual	Industry average	XXX2 Objective
Sales	100.0%	100.0%	100.0%	100.0%
Cost of Sales	80.0%	80.5%	81.8%	80.7%
Gross Profit	20.0%	19.5%	18.2%	19.3%
Total Expenses	17.9%	18.6%	14.7%	17.2%
Profit Before Taxes	2.1%	0.9%	3.5%	2.1%

In XXX2, Western Appliances' gross profit was 20.0% of sales. This represented an improvement over their XXX1 performance of 19.5%, the industry average of 18.2%, and their XXX2 objective of 19.3%. By any of these measures, this should be considered favorable. Apparently, they were able to control their purchasing costs and realize adequate prices in order to improve upon their own previous gross profit performance as well as the industry average.

Conflicts.

Sometimes financial analysis can lead to conflicting conclusions derived from identical facts. Comparing Western Appliances' 20.0% gross profit with the 18.2% industry average could raise questions. If Western Appliances were more competitive in its pricing, could it capture a larger market share? A reasonable answer to this question would depend upon thorough knowledge of their operations and the experience of their sales personnel in dealing with specific customers. Perhaps their pricing is fully competitive in their area or local retailers are willing to pay slightly more because of the superior services they offer. If this is the case, price cutting might only trim profit margins with no realistic hope of additional sales volume to offset the effects of the price reduction.

On the other hand, if their gross profit percentage is below that of the industry, a number of other questions would be raised, such as the following:

Are they purchasing at prices that are too high to provide an adequate gross profit?

Is their pricing structure so low that adequate gross profit margins cannot be attained?

Are salesmen too quick to cut prices?

Is their marketing effort too heavily concentrated in those product lines that offer a relatively low gross profit percentage?

Is their marketing effort directed toward those high-volume accounts that are so highly competitive that gross profit must be trimmed to an unrealistically low level?

Analysis of Sales Performance

The table shown below, analyzes the XXX2 sales of Western Appliances by account. Actual sales, gross profit, and the gross profit percentage are shown individually for major accounts and as a group for smaller accounts. These are reported on the bottom line and represent 50 small retailers served by Western Appliances.

WESTERN APPLIANCES, INC.
Sales Forecast, xxx3

Account	XXX2 Actual			XXX3 Forecast		
	Sales	Gross Profit	%	Sales	Gross Profit	%
Giant Discount	$ 300,000	$45,000	15.0	$323,500	$45,300	14.0
Appliance Mart	150,000	27,000	18.0	174,000	31,300	18.0
TV Center	120,000	21,600	18.0	159,000	23,900	15.0
Whitney Brothers	80,000	15,200	19.0	100,000	20,000	20.0
Packer Electronics	70,000	14,000	20.0	40,400	8,100	20.0
Consumers Outlet	40,000	7,200	18.0	50,000	9,000	18.0
Other (50stores)	440,000	110,000	25.0	553,100	142,400	25.7
Total	$1,200,000	$240,000	20.0	$1,400,000	$280,000	20.0

Let us consider Appliance Mart, one of the major accounts shown.

In XXX2, Western Appliances' sales to Appliance Mart were $150,000. These sales generated gross profit of $27,000, or 18.% of sales.

In XXX3, Western Appliances expects a general price increase of 5% with no change in the discount structure available to them from their suppliers.

Appliance Mart's business in XXX3 is expected to be affected only by general economic conditions such as the 5% price increase and an expected 10% industry growth in consumer demand for electrical appliances.

Appliance Mart operates a chain of discount stores in an economically stable suburban area. For XXX3, they have no plans to add or eliminate any stores. There are no changes expected in Western Appliances' relationship with them that would materially affect sales.

Therefore, the only factors affecting the sales forecast for Appliance Mart would be the planned 5% price increase and the general 10% increase in demand. Sales to Appliance Mart in XXX3 could then be forecast as follows:

This amount, $173,250, has been rounded to $174,000 and entered in the XXX3 sales forecast column.

Since there is no planned change in Western Appliances' discount structure from its suppliers, nor is there any indication that competition for Appliance Mart's business will be any more or less severe, Western Appliances probably should assume that gross profit as a percentage of these sales will remain at 18.0%, the XXX2 level. The gross profit expected on these sales could then be calculated as follows:

$174,000 x 0.180 = $31,320

This amount has been rounded to $31,300 and entered in the gross profit forecast column.

Subdividing Sales Categories

It is often useful to subdivide sales into more detailed classifications in order to develop a more precise forecast such as potential sales to a single customer. As an example, refer to the table below, Western Appliances' sales summary by product line to Giant Discount, its major customer in XXX2. Sales, gross profit, and the gross profit percentage are shown by product line so that each line may be considered separately to determine a realistic forecast for XXX3.

WESTERN APPLIANCES, INC.
Customer Sales Analysis - Giant Discount

Product line	XXX2 Actual			XXX3 Forecast		
	Sales	Gross profit	%	Sales	Gross profit	%
Television	$160,000	$16,000	10.0	$184,800	$18,500	10.0%
Automotive radios	20,000	6,000	30.0	--	--	--
Table radios	30,000	6,000	20.0	34,700	6,900	20.0
Stereo	40,000	7,000	18.0	46,200	8,300	18.0
Small appliances	50,000	10,000	20.0	57,800	11,600	20.0
Total	$300,000	$45,000	15.0%	$323,500	$45,300	14.0

Development of the XXX3 forecast will assume that Giant Discount's various stores are located in areas that are representative of the general economy and therefore will reflect the industry's expected sales growth of 10%; the price increase of 5% will have no significant effect on Giant Discount's sales; and competition among appliance wholesalers for Giant Discount's business will prevent Western Appliances from increasing its gross profit percentage in any product line.

The first product line on the table above, television sales, could then be forecast as follows:

XXX2 Sales	$160,000
+ 5% Price Increase	8,000
= Subtotal	$168,000
+ 10% Demand Increase	16,800
= Total	$184,800

Assuming that the gross profit percentage of 10.0% on television sales is maintained in XXX3, the forecast for gross profit can then be calculated as follows:

$184,800 x 0.100 = $18,480, rounded to $18,500

Giant Discount plans to discontinue its sales of

automotive radios in XXX3. Therefore, sales, gross profit, and the gross profit percentage for all are shown as zero on the table above.

Sales, gross profit, and gross profit percentages have all been determined for the remaining product lines and shown on the XXX3 forecast on the table above. You will note that the gross profit as a percentage of total sales in the XXX3 forecast, 14.0%, is well below the XXX2 experience of 15.0% even though the gross profit on each product line remains the same. This is due to the elimination of the highly profitable automotive radio line which produced a 30% gross profit but is being discontinued from Giant Discount's stores. In fact, the net effect of this discontinuation is that Western Appliances will realize additional gross profit of less than $1,000 on sales to Giant Discount despite a sales increase of almost $24,000. This important fact probably would not have been revealed if sales to Giant Discount had not been subdivided into individual product lines for analysis.

This negligible increase in gross profit will probably be more than offset by normal cost increases in various expense accounts required to handle Giant Discount's business in XXX3, At this point, the owners of Western Appliances would be well advised to take a hard look at their pricing strategy to see if more favorable prices can be realized in any product line without any significant sales loss so that the gross profit earned from this, its largest account, can be improved.

3. How to Develop Expense Budgets

After a realistic forecast has been developed for sales and gross profit, expenses for the coming year must be estimated in order to establish expense budgets and to determine expected operating profit.

Comparisons

As with the forecast of sales and gross profit, expense estimating begins with a review of the current year's performance based upon comparison with the following indicators:

Performance in prior periods

Industry averages

Objectives established for the current year

For purposes of comparison, it is often useful to express each expense as a percentage of total sales.

Comparing Variable Expenses

The use of percentages as a basis of comparison and forecasting is particularly applicable when analyzing variable expenses. Variable expenses are those that tend to change as a result of changes in sales volume. For example, if salesmen's commissions are based upon a percentage of sales, the total dollar amount of commissions earned would increase as sales increase. If sales in a month were 20% higher than expected, commissions paid would also increase 20% as a direct result of the higher sales volume.

Comparing Fixed Expenses

On the other hand, fixed expenses are not directly affected by short-term variations in sales volume. Therefore, a 20% increase in the dollar amount of any fixed expense such as salaries or rent would normally be considered unacceptable even if sales for the period increased by 20%. When comparing fixed expense levels with objectives or from one period to another, it is more realistic to make comparisons in absolute dollars rather than in percentages.

A business has sales and rent expense in January, February, and March as follows:

Month	Sales	Rent expense $	Rent expense % Sales
January	$100,000	$1,000	1.00
February	80,000	1,000	1.25
March	125,000	1,000	0.80

As a percentage of sales, rent expense was high in February and low in March. However, this does not indicate that control of this expense was more or less effective in either month. It simply reflects the changes in sales volume. In all three cases, the actual rent expense was 1,000.

Long-Range Considerations

Despite the shortcomings of using percentages to evaluate fixed expense control within the business from month to month, they can be useful when making long-term comparisons or comparisons with industry averages. These averages normally express expenses as percentages of sales, regardless of whether they are fixed or variable.

For example, assume that a business found that its rent expense as a percentage of sales was 2% compared with an industry average of 1%. This differential would have to be offset by better than average performance in gross profit or other expense classifications if the business expects to realize net profit equal to its industry average. Perhaps the reason for the high percentage is due to an exorbitant rental expense, or it may be caused by inadequate sales. In either case, certain questions must be answered. These could include the following:

Are we renting more space than we need?

Is our space too expensive for our requirements?

Could a less elaborate facility be located that would be adequate for our needs?

Would a less costly location be sufficient?

Is our space utilization inefficient?

Will expected sales increases be handled without renting additional space? Will this bring our rent expense percentage in line with the industry?

Can the terms of our lease be re-negotiated?

Similarly, when comparing long-term performance with prior periods, the use of fixed expense percentages can be helpful. For example, if you found that warehouse salaries jumped from 2% of sales to 4%, a number of important questions would be raised. These could include the following:

Are we now using too many warehouse personnel?

Are warehouse personnel less efficient?

Has ineffectiveness crept into the warehouse layout or operating procedure?

Are warehouse workers overpaid?

Is warehouse supervision inadequate?

Identifying Excessive Expenses

At Western Appliances, no objectives were available for XXX2 performance. Therefore, excessive expenses can be identified only by comparison with

XXX1 results, and, in some cases, with industry averages.

Industry Average Comparisons

Comparisons with industry averages are not available in all of Western Appliances' expense accounts. However, this can be determined by examining those accounts on the company's income statement that can be combined for comparison with industry averages. For example, the industry averages show that office salaries for the industry were 4.9% of sales. Examining the operating expense accounts at Western Appliances, the accounts that would appear to fall into this classification are the following:

Salary - Office Manager 1.4%

Salaries - Clerical 1.0%

Salaries - Warehouse 1.8%

The total of these expenses, 4.2% of sales, compares favorably with the industry average of 4.9%.

Comparison with Previous Periods

The information permits comparison of all expenses in XXX2 with XXX1 results.

The only variable expense at Western Appliances in XXX2 is salesmen's commissions. These represented 2.0% of sales in both XXX1 and XXX2. Therefore, they would not appear to be excessive.

In the fixed expense accounts, sharp increases could be noted in the following accounts and would warrant review and possible corrective action.

Account	XXX2	XXX1
Salary - Owner	$24,000	$20,000
Salaries - Warehouse	22,000	18,000
Salaries - Clerical	12,000	10,000
Employee Benefits	8,000	6,000
Utilities	4,000	3,000
Telephone	4,000	2,000
Supplies	2,000	1,000
Travel and Entertainment	13,000	10,000

Comparing Western Appliances' XXX2 fixed expenses with its experience in XXX1, significant increases are noted in almost every account. Some of these increases should be regarded with more concern than others and therefore given prompt attention. Reasons for the increases and possible corrective action must be determined.

Some increases were probably unavoidable, having been dictated by contract, legal requirements, or price increases beyond the company's control.

Others could probably be reduced with closer control. For example, travel and entertainment expense jumped from $10,000 to $13,000, an increase of $3,000. This sharp increase should indicate that a closer look at all travel and entertainment expenditures is in order to determine whether or not all were necessary. Could some have been avoided by restricting salesmen's expense accounts? Could more economical means of travel have been used? Could the company eliminate unnecessary trips that resulted in costs far beyond any real value to the business?

Supplies expense doubled from $1,000 to $2,000 although the volume of business increased by only about 10%. This sales increase would not seem to indicate a need for such a sharp increase in supplies usage. Such an expense could be controlled by closer attention to purchasing procedures and supplies issued to employees, use of less expensive supplies where possible, and so on.

Determining Expense Budgets

Budgets for each expense must be established, considering both external and internal factors, as in sales forecasting.

From the standpoint of expense budgeting, the following would be considered internal factors:

Corrective actions planned to bring excessive

expenses in line.

Policy changes such as new commission plans.

Commitments such as equipment purchases, leases on new facilities, or professional service contracts.

Planned salary increases.

Planned changes in benefit programs.

Additional personnel.

Promotional plans.

External factors could include the following:

Inflation and its effect on price increases from suppliers.

Tax rate increases including payroll taxes, local property taxes, inventory taxes, and so on.

Utility rate increases.

Additionally, the interrelated effects of expense increases must be considered. For example, payroll increases will increase payroll taxes and, possibly, employee benefits. Rent on larger facilities can also involve additional utilities expense.

Initial Forecast

The table below shows Western Appliances' initial forecast for XXX3 operating expenses.

The owner's salary will be increased from $24,000 to $26,000.

The office manager's salary will be increased from $17,000 to $18,000.

Salesmen's salaries will remain unchanged.

The expected sales increase will cause salesmen's commissions, 2% of sales, to increase from $24,000 to $28,000.

Warehouse salaries will be increased about 5% from $22,000 to $23,000.

Clerical salaries will be increased about 17% from $12,000 to $14,000.

Payroll taxes, approximately 8% of total compensation, will increase to $10,000 as a result of the compensation increases

Employee benefits expense is expected to increase from the present $8,000 to $9,000. This increase is dictated by increased premium costs for employees' health insurance.

Rent expense will increase from $9,000 to $10,000 due to a tax escalator clause in the lease agreement and a proposed municipal tax increase.

Utilities expense is expected to remain unchanged at $4,000.

Telephone expense is expected to be reduced from $4,000 to $3,000 because of tighter controls introduced by management in response to the sharp increase in XXX2.

New controls on supplies should hold this expense at $2,000 despite price increases.

To increase sales, the advertising and promotion budget will be increased from $13,000 to $15,000, a 20% increase.

Through tighter control, the owner expects to restrict travel and entertainment expense to the XXX2 level of $13,000 despite the general increase in travel-related costs.

Freight expense will increase from $16,000 to $18,000 reflecting the increased sales volume and higher freight tariffs.

Professional fees are expected to remain at $5,000.

Depreciation expense will increase from $6,000 to $8,000 due to the addition of new receiving equipment being purchased at a cost of $10,000 and depreciated over 5 years.

Total operating expenses will increase from $200,000 to $218,000. Profit before interest and taxes will be $62,000, an increase from $40,000 in XXX2.

WESTERN APPLIANCES, INC.
Sales And Expense Forecast
January 1 To December 31, XXX3

	XXX2 Actual	XXX2 (% sales)	XXX1 actual	XXX1 (% sales)	Industry (% Sales)	Revised XXX3 Forecast
Sales	$1,200,000	100.0%	$1,080,000	100.0%	100.00%	1,400,000
Cost of Sales	960,000	80.0%	880,000	81.5	81.8	1,120,000
Gross Profit	$240,000	20.0%	$200,000	18.5%	18.2%	280,000
Operating Expenses:						
Salary-Owner	$ 24,000	2.0%	$ 20,000	1.9%	1.7	26,000
Salary-Office Manager	17,000	1.4	16,000	1.5		18,000
Salaries-Salesmen	12,000	1.0	11,000	1.0		12,000
Commissions-Salesmen	24,000	2.0	22,000	2.0		28,000
Salaries-Warehouse	22,000	1.8	18,000	1.7		23,000
Salaries-Clerical	12,000	1.0	10,000	0.9		14,000
Payroll Taxes	9,000	0.8	8,000	0.7		10,000
Employee Benefits	8,000	0.7	6,000	0.6		9,000
Rent	9,000	0.8	9,000	0.8	0.7	10,000
Utilities	4,000	0.3	3,000	0.3		4,000
Telephone	4,000	0.3	2,000	0.2		3,000
Supplies	2,000	0.2	1,000	0.1		2,000
Advertising and Promotion	13,000	1.1	12,000	1.1		15,000
Travel and Entertainment	13,000	1.1	10,000	0.9		13,000
Freight	16,000	1.3	16,000	1.5		18,000
Professional Fees	5,000	0.4	4,000	0.4		5,000
Depreciation	6,000	0.5	5,000	0.5	0.5	8,000
Total Operating Expenses	$200,000	16.7%	$173,000	16.0%		$218,000
Profit Before						
Interest and Taxes	$40,000	3.3%	$27,000	2..6%		$62,000
Interest	15,000	1.3	12,000	1.1		17,000
Profit Before Income Taxes	$25,000	2.1%	$15,000	1.4%	2.5%	
Income Taxes	6,000	0.5	4,000	0.4		15,000
Net Profit	$19,000	1.6%	$11,000	1.1%		$30,000

4. Evaluating Your Performance

Once an initial plan has been established, it is often useful to review it in order to identify areas of further improvement.

In the example of Western Appliances, the expected profit before income taxes, 3.2% of sales ($46,000 : $1,400,000), is well above the industry average of 2.5% and no extensive reevaluation appears needed.

Too often, the owners of small businesses rely upon their eyes and ears to tell them whether or not the performance of their business is up to par. Unfortunately, our eyes and ears often betray us. The sales representative with the glib tongue and quick wit may appear to be your star performer while the facts, actual sales and profit, may show that someone else is doing a far better job. The secretary who constantly appears busy may be far less efficient than another who works in a more organized fashion with fewer errors and less need for duplicate effort.

There are also many aspects of a business that our eyes and ears cannot always sense. Changes in the market, shifts in customers' economic fortunes, and gradual but seemingly irreversible increases in costs can develop into crises unless they are detected at an early stage and effective action is taken promptly.

Performance Evaluation

The establishment of a profit plan permits you to evaluate performance in your business based upon facts, not upon random observations. Certainly, there is no substitute for the "gut feel" of the small business owner in making these important decisions that affect the prosperity of the business. However, the effectiveness of the owner's gut feel, when combined with facts, can dramatically increase the accuracy of management decisions.

Profit Plan

With a well-considered profit plan, out-of-line conditions can be detected at the earliest possible date. Corrective action can be taken promptly, eliminating the erosive effect of continuing losses as well as the need to react in a time of crisis. The profit plan also permits the owner to agree upon specific responsibilities with all employees who are in a position to influence sales or costs. Their performance can be evaluated and any deficiencies brought to their attention so that they can participate in the development of corrective action plans. As a further plus, the disciplined thinking about the future will permit you to foresee many problems before they occur and assist you in anticipating opportunities in your market that will permit you to build your business for greater sales and profit.

5. How To Be Pointed Toward Profit

Why do some business owner-managers hit the profit target more often than others? They do it because they keep their operation pointed in that direction - direction of profit making. They never lose sight of the goal - to finish the year with a profit.

This guide gives suggestions that should help an owner-manager to zero in on profit making. It points out that you must keep informed, make timely decisions, and take effective action. In effect you must control the activities of your company rather than being controlled by them.

A beginner rarely shoots a hole in one, hits a bull's-eye, or hooks a prize winning trout. Topnotch performance in golf, shooting, and fishing requires knowledge, practice, and perseverance.

Similarly, in small businesses, year-end profit comes to the owner-manager who strives for topnotch performance. You achieve profit making goals by knowing your operation, by practicing the art of making timely, balanced judgments and by controlling the company's activities.

Adapt the suggestions in this guide to your situation. They should help you call the shots to keep your company headed in the right direction - toward profit making.

First Rule of Profit Making: Know Your Business

The time-honored truth "Knowledge is power" is especially pertinent to the owner-manager of a small business. To keep your company pointed toward profit you must keep yourself well informed about it. You must know how the company is doing before you can improve its operation. You must know its weak points before you can correct them. Some of the knowledge you need you pick up from day-to-day personal observation, but records should be your principal source of information about profits, costs, and sales.

Know Your Profit. The profit and loss statement (or income statement) prepared regularly each month or each quarter by your accountant is one of the most vital indicators of your business's worth and health. You should make sure that this statement contains all the facts you need for evaluating your profit. This statement must pinpoint each revenue and cost area. For example, it should show the profit and loss for each of your products and product lines as well as the profit and loss for your entire operation.

It is a good idea to have your profit and loss statement prepared so that it shows each item for the current period, for the same period last year, and for the current year-to-date. For example, a

P&L statement for the month of November would show income and expenses for the current month, for November last year, and totals for the eleven months of the current year. Many corporations publish their annual reports with several previous years so stockholders can compare earnings.

Comparison is the key to using your P&L statement. If your accountant is not already furnishing figures that you can compare, you should discuss the possibility of having them provided.

Financial ratios from your balance sheet also help you to know if your profit is what it should be. For example, the ratio of net worth (return on investment ratio) shows what the business earned on the equity capital invested.

Know Your Costs. An owner-manager should know costs in detail. Then, you can compare your cost figures as a percentage of sales (operating ratio). Be certain that your costs are itemized so that you can put your fingers on those that seem to be rising or falling according to your experience and the cost figures of your industry. When costs are itemized, you can spot the culprit when the overall figure is higher than what you had budgeted. Take advertising costs for example. You can catch the offender if you break out your advertising expenditures by product lines and by media. In addition, a thorough check of inquiry returns from advertising will help to avoid unproductive publications.

In knowing your costs, keep in mind that the formula for profit is: Profit equals Sales minus Costs.

Know Your Product Markup. Be certain that the pricing of your products provides a markup adequate for the kind of profit you expect to achieve. You must keep constantly informed on pricing because you have to adjust for rising costs and at the same time keep prices competitive. Knowledge about your markup also helps you to run close outs with your eyes open. Continuing to make a product that only a few customers want is an effective merchandising tool only when you use it on purpose - for example, to hold or attract buyers for other high markup products. Don't hesitate to drop a loser from your line.

Garbage-In, Garbage-Out. An owner-manager should not fudge the records. The acronym GIGO that the computer industry uses is true with manually kept records as well as with machine-processed ones. If an owner-manager allows "garbage" to go into the records, the reports will contain "garbage." Reports need not be extensive but they must be accurate.

Look For Trends. Try not to look at a single month's sales or profit picture by itself. The figures on your operating statements are meaningful only when you put the picture in the right frame - that is, look at your figures in the context of what has happened and what is likely to happen. In that manner, you catch a downward trend before it gets out of hand.

You should also concern yourself with the figures behind the dollars - for example, the number of units sold or the number of orders. Insist on cost-per-unit statistics. The fluctuation of the cost-per-unit can be much more meaningful than just looking at the dollar figures alone. Another idea is to display these comparative figures on graphs so that significant trends can be seen easily.

Predict Your Future

Don't use a crystal ball to make forecasts of your business. By carefully analyzing the historic trends of your business, as shown in your records for the past five years, you can forecast for the year ahead. Your record of sales, your experience with the markets in which you sell, and your general knowledge of the economy should enable you to forecast a sales figure for the next year.

When you have a sales forecast figure, make up a budget showing your costs as a percentage of that figure. In the next year, you can compare actual P&L figures to your budgeted figures. Thus, your budget is an important tool for determining the health of your business.

Make Timely Decisions

Without action, forecasts and decisions about the future are not worth the paper they are written on. A decision that does not result in action is a poor one. The pace of business demands timely as well as informed decision making. If the owner-manager is to stay ahead of competition, you must move to control your destiny.

Effective decision making in the small business requires several things. The owner-manager must have as much accurate information as possible. With these facts, you should determine the consequences of all feasible courses of action and the time requirements. When you have made the judgment, you have set up your business so that the decisions you make can be transmitted into action.

Control Your Business

To be effective, the owner-manager must be able to motivate key people to get the results planned for within the cost and time limits allowed. In working to achieve results, the small business owner-manager has an advantage over big business. You can be fast and flexible while many large firms must await committee action before a decision is made. You do not have to get permission to act. And equally important, bottlenecks to implementing new practices can receive your personal attention.

One of the secrets is in deciding what items to control. Even in a small company, the owner-manager should not try to be all things to everyone. You should keep close control on people, products, money, and any other resources that you consider significant to keeping your operation pointed toward profit.

Manage Your People. Most businesses find that their largest expense is labor. Yet because of the close contact with employees, some owner-manager of small businesses do not pay enough attention to direct and indirect labor costs. They tend to think of these costs in terms of individuals rather than relate them to profit in terms of dollars and cents.

Here are a few suggestions concerning personnel management:

1. Periodically review each position in your company. Take a quarterly look at the job. Is work being duplicated? Is it structured so that it encourages the employee to become involved? Can the tasks be given to another employee or employees and a position eliminated? Can a part-time person fill the job.

2. Play a little private mental game. Imagine that you must get rid of one employee, If you had to let one person go, who would it be? How would you realign the jobs to make out? You may find a real solution to the imaginary problem is possible to your financial benefit.

3. Use compensation as a tool rather than viewing it as a necessary evil. Reward quality work. Investigate the possibility of using raises and bonuses as incentives for higher productivity. For example, can you schedule bonuses as morale boosters during seasonal slacks or other dull periods?

4. Remember that there are new ways of controlling absenteeism through incentive compensation plans. For example, the owner-manager of one small company eliminated vacations and sick leave. Instead, this owner-manager gave each employee thirty days annual leave to use as the employee saw fit. At the end of the year, the employees were paid at regular rates for the leave they didn't use. To qualify for the year-end pay, the employee had to prove that sick leave was taken only for that purpose. Non-sick leave had to be applied for in advance. As a result, unscheduled absences and overtime pay were reduced significantly. In addition, employees were happier and more productive than they were under the old system.

Control Your Inventory. Don't tie up all your money in inventory. Use a perpetual inventory system as a cost control rather than a system just for tax purposes. Establish use patterns or purchase patterns on the materials or items you must stock to keep the minimum number required to supply your customers or to maintain production. Excessive inventory, whether it is finished product or raw materials, ties up funds that could be used to better advantage, for example, to open up a new sales territory or to buy new machinery.

Centralize your purchases and avoid duplications. Be a comparative shopper. Confirm orders in writing. Get the price and amount straight right away.

Check what you receive for condition and quality. Check bills from suppliers against quotations. You do not want to be the victim of their error.

You should, however, keep one fact in mind when you set up your inventory control system. Do not spend more on the control system than it will return in savings.

Control Your Products. From control of inventory to control of products is but a step. Make sure that your sales people recognize the importance of selling the products that are the most profitable. Align your service policies with your markup in mind. Arrange your goods so that low markup items require the least handling.

Control Your Money. It is good policy to handle cash and checks as though they were perishable commodities. They are. Money in your safe earns no return; and it can be stolen. Bank promptly.

Use credit wisely and take advantage of discounts. One of the hallmarks of a successful business owner-manager is knowing how much credit you can afford to extend over any period and how much you have already extended. Grant credit willingly, but keep it on a systematic basis. Insist on a written credit application and see that the credit application contains a promise to pay according to the credit practice in your industry.

Get your monthly bills out to customers on time, and be certain that bills show date of purchases, what was purchased, how much it cost, and how much was paid, if anything, and then how much is owned. The statement should also show your customer any overdue balance and for how long it has been overdue.

Every account will not pay promptly but keep in mind that a slow paying customer can be profitable, especially if the customer buys large amounts of your high markup items. The danger is in letting such a customer get in beyond the ability to pay. Set up a system for collecting from late and slow paying accounts, but in reminding them to pay up, your objective is to get your money without losing their business.

Get Help When You Need It

It is good practice to use your outside advisors as you go along rather than calling on them only in emergencies. For example, your accountant can help you analyze the financial position of your business to help you avoid problems rather than to get you out of them.

Sometimes an owner-manager needs to call in a management consultant. For example, help may be needed in isolating and solving a problem that the owner-manager senses but can't quite put a finger on. In other instances, the consultant's professional background may be needed to supply skills that do not exist in the company - for example, the capability for doing market research or for setting up an inventory control system. In many cases, the management consultant can provide the time that the owner/manager lacks to implement a solution.

6. Using Financial Analysis to Increase Your Profits

Making a profit is the most important - some might say the only - objective of a business. Profit measures success. It can be defined simply: Revenues - Expenses = Profit. So, to increase profits you must raise revenues, lower expenses, or both. To make improvements you must know what's really going on financially at all times. You have to watch every financial event without any kind of optimistic filter.

This financial management analysis Guide is a series of questions with comments to help you analyze your profits, their sufficiency and trend, the contribution of each of your product lines or services to them, and to help you determine if you have the kind of record system you need. The questions and comments are not meant to be definitive presentations on the subjects. They are meant to point to areas where further study might be - well - profitable.

Are You making A Profit?

Financial Analysis of Revenues and Expenses

Since profit is revenues less expenses, to determine what your profit is you must first identify all revenues and expenses for the period under study.

1. Have you chosen an appropriate period for profit determination?

For accounting purposes firms generally use a twelve month period, such as January 1 to December 31 or July 1 to June 30. The accounting year you select doesn't have to be a calendar year (January to December); a seasonal business, for example, might close its year after the end of the season. The selection depends upon the nature of your business, your personal preference, or possible tax considerations.

2. Have you determined your total revenues for the accounting period?

In order to answer this question, consider the following questions:

What is the amount of gross revenue from sales of your goods or service? (Gross Sales)

What is the amount of goods returned by your customers and credited? (Returns and Rejects)

What is the amount of discounts given to your customers and employees? (Discounts)

What is the amount of net sales from goods and services? **(Net Sales** = Gross Sales - Returns and Rejects + Discounts))

What is the amount of income from other sources, such as interest on bank deposits, dividends from securities, rent on property leased to others? (Non-operating Income)

What is the amount of total revenue? (Total Revenue = Net Sales + Non-operating Income)

3. Do you know what your total expenses are?

Expenses are the cost of goods sold and services used in the process of selling goods or services. Some common expenses for all businesses are:

Cost of goods sold (Cost of Goods Sold = Beginning Inventory + Purchases - Ending Inventory)

Wages and salaries (Don't forget to include your own- at the actual rate - you'd have to pay someone else to do your job.)

Rent

Utilities (electricity, gas telephone, water, etc.)

Delivery expenses

Insurance

Advertising and promotional costs

Maintenance and upkeep

Depreciation (Here you need to make sure
your depreciation policies are realistic and that
all depreciable items are included)

Taxes and licenses

Interest

Bad debts

Professional assistance (accountant, attorney,
etc.)

There are of course, many other types of expenses,
but the point is that every expense must be
recorded and deducted from your revenues before
you know what your profit is. Understanding your
expenses is the first step toward controlling them
and increasing your profit.

Financial Ratios

A financial ratio is an expression on the relationship
between two items selected from the income
statement or the balance sheet. Ratio analysis helps
you evaluate the weak and strong points in your
financial and managerial performance.

4. Do you know your current ratio?

The current ratio (current assets divided by current debts) is a measure of the cash or near cash position (liquidity) of the firm. It tells you if you have enough cash to pay your firm's current creditors. The higher the ratio, the more liquid the firm's position is and, hence, the higher the credibility of the firm. Cash, receivables, marketable securities, and inventory are current assets. Naturally you need to be realistic in valuing receivable and inventory for a true picture of your liquidity, since some debts may be un-collectable and some stock obsolete. Current liabilities are those which must be paid in one year.

5. Do you know your quick ratio?

Quick assets are current assets minus inventory. The quick ratio (or acid-test ratio) is found by dividing quick assets by current liabilities. The purpose, again, is to test the firm's ability to meet its current obligations. This test doesn't include inventory to make it a stiffer test of the company's liquidity. It tells you if the business could meet its current obligations with quickly convertible assets should sales revenue suddenly cease.

6. Do you know your total debt to net worth ratio?

This ratio (the result of total debt divided by net worth then multiplied by 100) is a measure of how company can meet its total obligation from equity. The lower the ratio, the higher the proportion of equity relative to debt and the better the firm's credit rating will be.

7. Do you know your average collection period?

You find this ratio by dividing accounts receivable by daily credit sales. (Daily credit sales = annual credit sales divided by 360.) This ratio tells you the length of time it takes the firm to get its cash after making a sale on credit. The shorter this period the quicker the cash flow is. A longer than normal period may mean overdue and un-collectible bills. If you extend credit for a specific period (say, 30 days), this ratio should be very close to the same number of day. If it's much longer than the established period, you may need to alter your credit policies. It's wise to develop an aging schedule to gauge the trend of collections (without adequate financing charges) hurt your profit, since you could be doing something much more useful with your money, such as taking advantage of discounts on your own payables.

8. Do you know your ratio of net sales to total assets?

This ratio (net sales divided by total assets) measures the efficiency with which you are using your assets. A higher than normal ratio indicates that the firm is able to generate sales from its assets faster (and better) than the average concern.

9. Do you know your operating profit to net sales ratio?

This ratio (the result of dividing operating profit by net sales and multiplying by 100) is most often used to determine the profit position relative to sales. A higher than normal ratio indicates that your sales are good, that your expenses are low, or both. Interest income and interest expense should not be included in calculating this ratio.

10. Do you know your net profit to total assets ratio?

This ratio (found by multiplying by 100 the result of dividing net profit by total assets) is often called return on investment or ROI. It focuses on the profitability of the overall operation of the firm. Thus, it allows management to measure the effects of its policies on the firm's profitability. The ROI is the single most important measure of a firm's financial position. You might say it's the bottom line for the bottom line.

11. Do you know your net profit to net worth ratio?

This ratio is found by dividing net profit by net worth and multiplying the result by 100. It provides information on the productivity of the resources the owners have committed to the firm's operations.

All ratios measuring profitability can be computed either before or after taxes, depending on the purpose of the computations. Ratios have limitations. Since the information used to derive ratios is itself based on accounting rules and personal judgments, as well as facts, the ratios cannot be considered absolute indicators of a firm's financial position. Ratios are only one means of assessing the performance of the firm and must be considered in perspective with many other measures. They should be used as a point of departure for further analysis and not as an end in themselves.

Sufficiency Of Profit

The following questions are designed to help you measure the adequacy of the profit your firm is making. Making a profit is only the first step; making enough profit to survive and grow is really what business is all about.

12. Have you compared your profit with your profit goals?

13. Is it possible your goals are too high or too low?

14. Have you compared your present profits (absolute and ratios) with the profits made in the last one to three years?

15. Have you compared your profits (absolute and ratios) with profits made by similar firms in your line?2

A number of organizations publish financial ratios for various businesses, among them Dun & Bradstreet. Robert Morris Associates, the Accounting Corporation of America, NCR Corporation, and the Bank of America. Your own trade association may also publish such studies. Remember, these published ratios are only averages. You probably want to be better than average.

Trend Of Profit

16. Have you analyzed the direction your profits have been taking?

The preceding analysis, with all their merits, report on a firm only at a single time in the past. It is not possible to use these isolated moments to indicate the trend of your firm's performance. To do a trend analysis performance indicators (absolute amounts or ratios) should be computed for several time periods (yearly for several years, for example) and the results laid out in columns side by side for easy comparison. You can then evaluate your performance, see the direction it's taking, and make initial forecasts of where it will go.

17. Does your firm sell more than one major product line or provide several distinct services?

If it does, a separate profit and ratio analysis of each should be made:

To show the relative contribution by each product line or service;

To show the relative burden of expenses by each product or service;

To show which items are most profitable, which are less so, and which are losing money; and

To show which are slow and fast moving.

Mix Of Profit

The profit analysis of each major item help you find out the strong and weak areas of your operations. They can help you to make profit-increasing decisions to drop a product line or service or to place particular emphasis behind one or another.

Records

Good records are essential. Without them a firm doesn't know where it's been, where it is, or where it's heading. Keeping records that are accurate, up-to-date, and easy to use is one of the most important functions of the owner-manager, his or her staff, and his or her outside counselors (lawyer, accountant, banker).

Basic Records

18. Do you have a general journal and/or special journals, such as one for cash receipts and disbursements?

A general journal is the basic record of the firm. Every monetary event in the life of the firm is entered in the general journal or in one of the special journals.

19. Do you prepare a sales report or analysis?

(a)., Do you have sales goals by product, department, and accounting period (month, quarter, year)?

(b)., Are your goals reasonable?

(c)., Are you meeting your goals?

If you aren't meeting your goals, try to list the likely reasons on a sheet of paper. Such a study might include areas such as general business climate, competition, pricing, advertising, sales promotion, credit policies, and the like. Once you've identified the apparent causes you can take steps to increase sales (and profits).

Buying and Inventory System

20. Do you have a buying and inventory system?

The buying and inventory systems are two critical areas of a firm's operation that can affect profitability.

21. Do you keep records on the quality, service, price, and promptness of delivery of your sources of supply?

22. Have you analyzed the advantages and disadvantages of:

(a) Buying from several suppliers,

(b) Buying from a minimum number of suppliers?

23. Have you analyzed the advantages and disadvantages of buying through cooperatives or other systems?

24. Do you know:

(a) How long it usually takes to receive each order?

(b) How much inventory cushion (usually called safety stock) to have so you can maintain normal sales while you wait for the order to arrive?

25. Have you ever suffered because you were out of stock?

26. Do you know the optimum order quantity for each item you need?

27. Do you (or can you) take advantage of quantity discounts for large size single purchases?

28. Do you know your costs of ordering inventory and carrying inventory?

The more frequently you buy (smaller quantities per order), the higher your average ordering costs (clerical costs, postage, telephone costs etc.) will be, and the lower the average carrying costs (storage, loss through pilferage, obsolescence, etc.) will be. On the other hand, the larger the quantity per order, the lower the average ordering cost and the higher the carrying costs. A balance should be struck so that the minimum cost overall for ordering and carrying inventory can be achieved.

29. Do you keep records of inventory for each item?

These records should be kept current by making entries whenever items are added to or removed from inventory. Simple records on 3 x 5 or 5 x 7 cards can be used with each item being listed on a separate card. Proper records will show for each item: quantity in stock, quantity on order, date of order, slow or fast seller, and valuations (which are important for taxes and your own analyses.)

Other Financial Records

30. Do you have an accounts payable ledger?

This ledger will show what, whom, and why you owe. Such records should help you make your payments on schedule. Any expense not paid on time could adversely affect your credit, but even more importantly such records should help you take advantage of discounts which can help boost your profits.

31. Do you have an accounts receivable ledger?

This ledger will show who owes money to your firm. It shows how much is owed, how long it has been outstanding and why the money is owed. Overdue accounts could indicate that your credit granting policy needs to be reviewed and that you may not be getting the cash into the firm quickly enough to pay your own bills at the optimum time.

32. Do you have a cash receipts journal?

This journal records the cash received by source, day, and amount.

33. Do you have a cash payments journal?

This journal will be similar to the cash receipts journal but will show cash paid out instead of cash received. The two cash journals can be combined, if convenient.

34. Do you prepare an income (profit and loss or P&L) statement and a balance sheet?

These are statements about the condition of your firm at a specific time and show the income, expenses, assets, and liabilities of the firm. They are absolutely essential.

35. Do you prepare a budget?

You could think of a budget as a "record in advance," projecting "future" inflows and outflows for your business. A budget is usually prepared for a single year, generally to correspond with the accounting year. It is then, however broken down into quarterly and monthly projections.

There are different kinds of budget: cash, production, sales, etc. A cash budget, for example, will show the estimate of sales and expenses for a particular period of time. The cash budget forces the firm to think ahead by estimating its income and expenses. Once reasonable projections are made for every important product line or department, the owner-manager has set targets for employees to meet for sales and expenses. You must plan to assure a profit. And you must prepare a budget to plan.

7. Additional Profits Through Management Planning and Goal Setting

Many authorities on business management identify five functions of management:

planning,

organizing,

directing,

controlling, and

coordinating.

Management Business planning and controlling functions often get less attention from owner-managers of businesses than they should. One way to strengthen both of these functions is through effective goal setting.

Long range goals for sales, profits, competitive position, development of people, and industrial relations must be established. Then, goals are set for the current year which will lead towards the accomplishment of the long range goals.

This guide presents Management by Objectives to the owner-manager of a company for use in this type of management business planning and goal setting. MBO includes goal setting by all managers down to the first level of supervision. Their goals are tied to those of the company.

Traditionally, people have worked according to job descriptions that list the activities of the job. The Management by Objectives (MBO) approach, on the other hand, stresses results.

Let's look at an example. Suppose that you have a credit manager and that his or her job description simply says that the credit manager supervises the credit operations of the company. The activities of the credit manager are then listed. Under MBO, the credit manager could have five or six goals covering important aspects of the work. One goal might be to increase credit sales enough to support a 15 percent increase in sales.

The traditional job description for a personnel specialist might include language about conducting the recruiting program for your company. Under MBO, the specialist's work might be covered in five or six goals - one which could be "recruit five new employees in specified categories by July 1."

Thus, MBO looks for results, not activities. With MBO, you view the job in terms of what it should achieve. Activity is never the essential element. It is merely an intermediate step leading to the desired result.

What Business Am I In?

In making long range plans, the first question you ought to think about is "what business am I in?" Is the definition you have of your business is right for today's market?

Are there emerging customer needs that will require a changed definition of your business next year?

For example, one owner-manager's business was making metal trash cans. When sales began to fall off, the owner was forced to reexamine the business. To regain lost sales and continue to grow the owner redefined the product as metal containers and developed a marketing plan for that product.

How you view your business will provide the framework for your planning with respect to markets, product development, buildings and equipment, financial needs, and staff size.

Your long range objectives for your business will be the cornerstone in the MBO program for your company. At a minimum, they must be clearly communicated to your managers; however, for a truly vital program your managers should have a part in formulating these long range goals. Your managers will base their short range goals on these objectives. If they have had a role in establishing the long range objectives, they will be more committed to achieving them.

The Complete MBO Program

Management by Objectives may be used in all kinds of organizations. But not everyone has had the same degree of success in using this concept. From examining those MBO programs that failed, it is clear that the programs were incomplete.

The minimum requirements for an MBO program are:

Each manager's job includes five to ten goals expressed in specific, measurable terms.

Each manager reporting to you proposes his or her goals to you in writing. When you both agree on each goal, a final written statement of the goal is prepared.

Each goal consists of the statement of the goal, how it will be measured, and the work steps necessary to complete it.

Results are systematically determine at regular intervals (at least quarterly) and compared with the goals.

When progress towards goals is not in accordance with your plans, problems are identified and corrective action is taken.

Goals at each level of management are related to the level above and the level below.

Goal Setting

Goals for each of your managers are the crucial element in any MBO system. Goals at middle level of management must be consistent with those at top levels. Goals of first line supervisors must relate to those at middle levels. Goals prepared by the manager responsible for certain steps in a large processing operation must tie in with those of managers responsible for other steps in the processing. And all goals must relate to and support your long range objectives for the company.

When all these goals are consistent, then an MBO system will be developed. Until then, there will be many like the middle manager of a research and development company who exclaimed in a seminar, "How can I set my goals when I don't know where top management wants to go?"

Each manager will probably find between five and eight goals enough to cover those aspects of the job crucial to successful performance. These are the elements which you will use to judge his or her performance. Of course, other duties which do not fall into the above goals should not be neglected. But they are of secondary importance.

When you first start your MBO program, your managers will undergo a learning period. They must learn how to prepare a goal which will make them stretch but is not beyond their capabilities. They must learn to develop ways to effectively measure real problems which threaten the achievement of the goals and then take steps to cope with the problems.

During this learning period, your managers should first set a few goals. Then as they learn how to develop and achieve goals, the coverage and number of goals can be extended.

The Miniature Work Plan

Your managers may find the miniature work plan useful. On this work plan the manager can show each of the major work steps (sub-goals) necessary to reach the goal. Then, if each work step is performed by the indicated date, the goal will be reached when the last work step is completed.

You may also use this form to discuss goals with your manager. By looking at this form, you can see not only the goal but also the plan for reaching that goal. This will allow you to ask questions about the work steps and anticipated problems, as well as to question how the goal will be measured. By pointing out the relationship between the manager's goal and your goal, you'll be helping each of your managers to understand how his/her goals relate to those of the company.

A Manager's Goal

Instructions for Completing Form

Management by Objectives provides for the establishment of four to ten goals by each manager. You should set up goals in each of several important areas in your job. You might try to establish at least one in each of these categories: Regular, Problem Solving, Innovative, and Development. By following this approach you will be more likely to see the full range of possibilities open to you through goal setting.

Develop each goal as a miniature work plan. The steps that follow will result in goals which are complete and useful to both you and your boss.

Goal (Be specific and concise)

_____

Measurement (The bench mark that tells you that you have achieved the goal, should be expressed in quantitative terms)

_____

Problems Anticipated

_____

_____

_____

Work Steps (List three or four most essential steps, give completion dates for each)

_____

_____

_____

Superior's Goal (Give goal at next higher level to which your goal relates).

_____

_____

Whenever a problem is listed on the work plan, the manager should include a work step to deal with it. For example, suppose the head of your supply department set a goal to deliver all packages within one day of when they were received. He thought he might have difficulty in getting his people to follow the new procedures. So, he included a work step to teach these procedures before the new program went into effect.

Kinds of Goals

When your managers begin to set their goals, they may want to know what areas are suitable for goal setting. What are the really important aspects of their jobs rather than that part which is most visible to them? How can they be sure that their program is balanced for the long haul, rather than just reacting to immediate, pressing problems? How can they set goals which are most likely to help them control their jobs?

It might be useful for them to have a classification of goals that suggests areas of opportunity. Generally, each manager should have between five and eight goals. One or two goals in each of these areas should be helpful:

1. Regular work goals.

2. Problem solving goals.

3. Innovative goals.

4. Development goals.

Regular work refers to those activities which make up the major part of the manager's responsibilities. The head of production would be primarily concerned with the amount, quality, and efficiency of production. The head of marketing would be primarily concerned with developing and conducting the market research and sales programs. Each manager should be able to find opportunities to operate more efficiently, to improve the quality of the product or service, and to expand the total amount produced or marketed.

Problem solving goals will give your managers an opportunity to define their major problems. There is no danger of anyone ever running out of problems. New problems or new versions of old problems always seem to replace those overcome.

Innovative goals may be viewed the same way. A goal for innovation may apply to an actual problem. But, some innovation may not deal with a problem. For example, the head of building management sets a goal to invigorate the employee suggestion program by putting five suggestions into effect during the next four months. There was no specific to be solved, the manager was just trying to do the best job possible.

The development goal recognizes how important the development of your employees is to your business. Your managers can be encouraged to develop their people just as they are to produce more effectively. Every manager must be to some extent a teacher and a coach; each manager must plan for the employees' continued growth in both technical area and in working together effectively.

By asking your managers to set at least one goal in the four areas listed above, you may open their eyes to possibilities they had not seen before. the goal setting process can be a very useful educational step, even for those who are primarily specialists.

Progress Reports

An MBO program without provision for regular reports on progress is worthless. That is why some articles and books on MBO call the concept MBO/R. The "R" refers to results. Nothing is accomplished by setting goals or objectives unless the program calls for a regular review of progress towards results.

A large organization issued nearly 100 pages of goals prepared by many of its managers. Most of the goals were well developed. The document was very impressive. But there was absolutely no provision for a reporting system of any kind. It is easy to imagine the reaction of those who set goals for the first year when they were asked the following year to draw up new goals.

A monthly or quarterly review of progress towards goals will help you determine where progress is below expectations. For example, suppose that one of your goals calls for a reduction of overtime by 50 percent this year, and the first quarter reduction is only 15 percent. A special effort must be exerted in the succeeding quarters to regain the lost ground or the goal will not be achieved by the end of the year. When progress is below expectations, the problem or problems holding back progress should be identified and assigned to someone, usually the manager, for resolution. Make these assignments part of the company MBO files so that responsibility for correcting the problem areas cannot be evaded.

Performance Evaluation

You will have to evaluate the performance of every person working for you in some way, either formally or informally. When your managers are working to achieve a full set of five to eight goals, their ability to get results on each goal can be a good, objective measure of performance.

Traditional performance evaluation systems have been strongly criticized because they deal with subjective matters such as leadership qualities, rather than the more objective measure of results. Evaluating performance by MBO, while objective, is a complex task, which must be undertaken with care by someone who fully understands MBO. Failure to reach goals can be a result of setting the wrong objectives in the first place, the existence of organizational restrictions not taken into account, inadequate or improper measures of goal achievement, personal failure, or a combination of factors.

Installing MBO

When installing an MBO program, many owner-managers have found it best to start their jobs by asking their managers to define their jobs. What are their major responsibilities? Then, for each responsibility, the manager and the boss decide how they will measure performance in terms of results.

The result of this exercise may surprise you. Often managers and their bosses do not even agree on the manager's major responsibilities. Also, you may find that no one is performing some of the functions that you consider important.

As the owner-manager, you must appreciate what the system will do. You have to show interest in the concept from the beginning. You have to set the example for your subordinate managers, if the MBO system is to be a success

The education of your managers may be a formidable task. They have probably thought in terms of specific functions - managing a sales department, directing a credit office - rather than in terms of goals which contribute to the organization.

It might be best to start with a seminar of six to nine hours in a classroom. This ought to be enough to introduce MBO to the managers who will be setting goals. Either you or a consultant might conduct the seminar. (If you choose a consultant, be sure that you are there for the entire seminar).

Provide enough time so that your managers can express their doubts, reservations or opposition to MBO. It is best to get their feelings out into the open as soon as possible. Other participants can help them deal with their concerns.

A very useful part of such a seminar is the preparation of an actual goal by each participant. In small group sessions, your mangers can help each other by reviewing work plans and offering suggestions to improve each others plans.

Working with goal setting, periodic review of goals, and other aspects of MBO will be a learning experience for most managers. If they set annual goals, it may take three to four years before good results from this system of managing appear. MBO may look simple on the surface, but it requires experience and skill to make it work effectively.

Threats to the MBO System

Not all MBO programs are successful. Some of the leading reasons why past programs failed to reach their potential are:

1. Top management did not get involved.

2. Corporate objectives were inadequate.

3. MBO was installed as a crash program.

4. It was difficult to learn the system because the nature of MBO was not taught.

It is hard to get people to think in terms of results rather than activities relating to their work. However, it can be done. The sequence of steps one owner-manager uses may not work for another. It is often an individual matter. Results are what count.

If you feel that you are ready to introduce MBO to your company, why not set this as a goal for yourself. Turn back and follow through the work plan. List your goal, measurement, anticipated problems, and the work steps necessary to get your company managing by objectives.

8. How to Cut Costs in Your Business

Increasing profits through reduce costs and cost cutting must be based on the concept of an organized, planned program. Unless adequate records are maintained through a proper accounting system, there can be no basis for ascertaining and analyzing costs.

Cost cutting is not simply attempting to slash any and all expenses unmethodically. The owner-manager must understand the nature of expenses

and how expenses inter-relate with sales, inventories, cost of goods sold, gross profits, and net profits.

Reduce costs does not mean only the reduction of specific expenses. You can achieve greater profits through more efficient use of the expense dollar. Some of the ways you do this are by increasing the average sale per customer, by effectively using display space and thereby increasing sales volume per square foot, by getting a larger return for your advertising and sales promotion dollar, and by improving your internal methods and procedures.

Profit is in danger when good merchandising and cost control do not go hand in hand. A big sales volume does not necessarily mean a big profit, as one retailer, Carl Jones, learned.

Jones's pride was stocking stylish and well assorted lines of merchandise. Each year, sales volume increased. This increase was attributed to good merchandise which Jones felt took care of the steady rise in expenses.

But Mr. Jones began to have doubts when he found it necessary to get bank loans more often than had been his practice. When he discussed the problem with his banker, Jones was advised to check expenses. As the banker said, "A large and increasing sales volume often creates the appearance of prosperity while behind-the-scene expenses are eating up the profit."

Paying The Right Price

Your goal should be to pay the right price for prosperity. Determining that price for your operation goes beyond knowing what your expenses are. Reducing expenses to increase profit requires you to obtain the most efficient use of the expense dollar.

Look, for example, at the payroll expense. Salesclerks are paid to sell goods, and their productivity is the key to reducing the payroll cost.

If you train a salesclerk to make multiple sales at higher unit prices, you increase productivity and your profits without adding dollars to your payroll expenses. Or, if four salesclerks can be trained to sell the amount previously sold by seven, the payroll can be cut by three persons.

An understanding of the worth of each expense item comes from experience and an analysis of records. Adequate records tell what has happened. Their analysis provide facts which can help you set realistic goals, you are paying the right price for your store's prosperity.

Analyze Your Expenses

Sometimes you cannot cut an increase item. But you can get more from it and thus increase your profits. In analyzing your expenses, you should use percentages rather than actual dollar amounts.

For example, if you increase sales and keep the dollar amount of an expense the same, you have decreased that expense as a percentage of sales. When you decrease your cost percentage, you increase your percentage of profit.

On the other hand, if your sales volume remains the same, you can increase the percentage of profit by reducing a specific item of expense. Your goal, of course, is to do both: to decrease specific expenses and increase their productive worth at the same time.

Before you can determine whether cutting expenses will increase profits, you need information about your operation. This information can be obtained only if you have an adequate recordkeeping system. Such records will provide the figures to prepare a profit and loss statement (preferably monthly for most retail businesses), a budget, break-even calculations, and evaluations of your operating ratios compared with those of similar types of business.

Break-even

A useful method for making expense comparisons is break-even analysis. Break-even is the point at which gross profit equals expenses. In a business year, it is the time at which your sales volume has become sufficient to enable your over-all operation to start showing a profit.

Once your sales volume reached the break-even point, your fixed expenses are covered. Beyond the break-even point, every dollar of sales should earn you an equivalent additional profit percentage.

It is important to remember that once sales pass the break-even point, the fixed expenses percentage goes down as the sales volume goes up. Also the operating profit percentage increases at the same rate as the percentage rate for fixed expenses decreases - provided, of course, that variable expenses are kept in line.

Locating Reducible Expenses

Your profit and loss (or income) statement provides a summary of expense information and is the focal point in locating expenses that can be cut. Therefore, the information should be as current as possible. As a report of what has already been spent, a P and L statement alerts you to expense items that bear watching in the present business period. If you get a P and L statement only at the end of the year, you should consider having one prepared more often. At the end of each quarter might be often enough for some firms. Ideally, you can get the most recent information from a monthly P and L.

Regardless of the frequency, for the most information two P and L statements should be prepared. One statement should report the sales, expenses, profits and/or loss of your operations cumulatively for the current business year to date. The other should report on the same items for the last complete month or quarter. Each of the statements should also carry the following information:

(1) this year's figures and each item as a percentage of sales.

(2) last year's figures and the percentages.

(3) the difference between last year and this year - over or under.

(4) budgeted figures and the respective percentages.

(5) the difference between this year and the budgeted figures - over and under.

(6) average percentages for your line of business (industry operating ratio) when available, and

(7) the difference between your annual percentages and the industry ratios - under or over.

This information allows you to locate expense variation in three ways: (1) by comparing this year to last year, (2) by comparing expenses to your own budgeted figures, and (3) by comparing your percentages to the operating ratios for your line of business. The important basis for comparison is the percentage figure. It represents a common denominator for all three methods. When you have indicated the percentage variations, you should then study the dollar amounts to determine what line of operative action is needed.

Because your cost cutting will come largely form variable expenses, you should make sure that they are flagged on your P and L statements. Variable expenses are those which fluctuate with the increase or decrease of sales volume. Some of them are: advertising, delivery, wrapping supplies, sales salaries, commissions, and payroll taxes. Fixed expenses are those which stay the same regardless of sales volume. Among them are: your salary, salaries for permanent non-selling employees (for example, the bookkeeper), depreciation, rent, and utilities.

Taking cost cutting Action

When you have located a problem expense area, the next step obviously is to reduce that cost so as to increase your profit. A key to the effectiveness of your cost-cutting action is the worth of the various expenditures. As long as you know the worth of your expenditures, you can profit by making small improvements in expenses. Keep an open eye and an open mind. It is better to do a spot analysis once a month than to wait several months and then do a detailed study. Take action as soon as possible. You can refine your cost-cutting action as you go along.